Michael & Kirk
Douglas

by

Skip Press

CRESTWOOD HOUSE
Parsippany, New Jersey

Library of Congress Cataloging-in-Publication Data
Press, Skip, 1950–
    Michael & Kirk Douglas / by Skip Press. — 1st ed.
      p.   cm. — (Star families)
    Includes index.
    ISBN 0-89686-880-X   pbk 0-382-24941-0
    1. Douglas, Michael, 1944–   —Juvenile literature. 2. Douglas, Kirk, 1916–   —Juvenile literature. 3. Motion picture
actors and actresses—United States—Biography—Juvenile literature. [1. Douglas, Michael, 1944– . 2. Douglas, Kirk, 1916–
3. Actors and actresses.] I. Title. II. Series.
PN2287.D5425P74   1995
791.43'028'092273—dc20
[B]   94-28650
Summary: A joint biography on the legendary Kirk Douglas and his famous son, Michael.

Photo Credits
All photos courtesy of AP—Wide World Photos.

Acknowledgments

The author would like to thank the following people for their contributions in compiling this book:

Annene Kaye and Jim Sclavunos, authors of *Michael Douglas and the Douglas Clan: An Intimate Look at Two Generations of Hollywood Superstars*. New York: Knightsbridge Publishing Company, 1990.

Michael Munn, author of *Kirk Douglas: A Biography*. New York: St. Martin's Press, 1985.

Kirk Douglas, author of *The Ragman's Son*. New York: Pocket Books, 1988.

Liz Smith of the *New York Daily News*, Bob Strauss of the *Los Angeles Daily News*, Dennis Davidson & Associates, and David Fox of the *Los Angeles Times*.

Published by Crestwood House, an imprint of Silver Burdett Press.
A Simon & Schuster Company.
299 Jefferson Road, Parsippany, NJ 07054

Produced by Great Flying Fish/Spicer, MN

Printed in the United States of America

10 9 8 7 6 5 4 3 2 1

Contents

Kirk Douglas joins his son as Michael receives his first Academy Award.

"Bad Guys" Make Good

On April 11, 1988, actor Michael Douglas stood before his fellow filmmakers to accept their highest award. The Academy of Motion Picture Arts and Sciences was awarding Michael an Oscar for his portrayal of super-rich villain Gordon Gekko in the movie *Wall Street*. It was not the first Oscar Michael had received, but it was his first one for acting. Michael began his acceptance speech by telling the audience and the millions of fans watching on TV that the role was one not many people thought he could play. Gordon Gekko was the first bad-guy role Michael had ever played. Until then, he had always been seen on-screen as a good guy. His characters usually got themselves into lots of trouble, but audiences still cheered for them to win.

"I'd like to dedicate this award to my parents and stepparents, who have been supportive over the years," Michael told the audience at the **Academy Awards** ceremony, "and particularly to my father, who I don't think ever missed one of my college productions, for his continued support, and in particular for helping his son step out of his shadow. I'll be eternally grateful to you, Dad."

Michael looked at the TV camera and said good-night to his young son, Cameron, who was watching at home. Michael thanked Diandra Douglas, his wife, who was crying happy tears in the audience. But he had to wait to thank his father personally. His famous actor father, Kirk Douglas, had always played tough guys in the movies. Kirk hadn't been tough enough to come to the Academy Awards ceremony, though. He had been nervous that Michael might lose to one of the other Oscar nominees!

After the awards ceremony, Michael and Diandra attended a party at the Beverly Hills home of Kirk and Anne Douglas. As Kirk held his son's Best Actor Oscar, he might have been a little sad. After all, Kirk had been nominated for the Best Actor Oscar three times, yet each time had failed to win.

Michael had appeared in 19 movies before winning the Best Actor Oscar. When he got his first nomination, Kirk had appeared in only 8 films. He received two more nominations in the next four years, but the last one had been in 1956. It was unlikely that Kirk would ever be nominated again.

Although he had never won an Oscar, Kirk had good reason to feel satisfied with his life. By 1988, he had appeared in 75 movies, and had traveled the world making them. He had also toured the globe as a goodwill ambassador for the U.S. government. He had a happy home life, and his four sons were all successful. Michael was a superstar film producer and actor. Joel, Peter, and Eric were respected film executives.

And only a few months before Michael's Oscar win, Kirk had also received a big honor. The school where he had perfected his acting, the **American Academy of Dramatic Arts** in New York City, gave Kirk its **Lifetime Achievement Award**. All four sons were at the ceremony to help their father celebrate.

Michael told the audience at Kirk's ceremony how proud he was to be Kirk Douglas's son. "My father always wanted to be an actor," Michael said, "and it's amazing to see all the roles he's played. He's played a soldier, a painter, a Viking, architect, boxer, and many others . . . . But of all the roles he's played, I want to congratulate him publicly on his role as a father."

6   Kirk Douglas won the American Academy of Dramatic Arts' Lifetime Achievement Award in 1991.

Later, when asked by a *New York Times* reporter about Michael's success, Kirk said Michael's achievements made him feel immortal. He summed up his response this way: "Hey—I'm not such a bad guy." Michael's accomplishments helped Kirk make peace with himself, the proud father announced.

With this kind of love from his sons, how could Kirk Douglas possibly consider himself to be a bad guy? He was rich, internationally famous, and in good health. At the time of his Lifetime Achievement Award, he had been happily married for 34 years. He had also written his autobiography, *The Ragman's Son*, which would go on to become a **number one best-seller**. Sure, he had *played* a large number of bad guys in his film roles, but his credits included a lot more heroes. Why the self-doubt? Was it because he had never won an Oscar?

Kirk celebrates with his sons after receiving his Lifetime Achievement Award.

From Rags to Broadway

Columnist Liz Smith of the *New York Daily News* called Kirk Douglas's autobiography "one of the best life stories ever written." *People* magazine described the book as a "heart-stirring story of the American Dream come true." Kirk himself said his life was like a "B movie"—that is, a tale people might find corny or hard to believe. Nevertheless, his amazing story is not only true but an inspiration.

Kirk's family name was originally Danielovitch. Kirk's father, Herschel, was an **illiterate** peasant who had fled Russia in 1908 to keep from being drafted into the army. Bryna, Kirk's mother, came from a family of Ukrainian farmers. Although she was uneducated, she had a vivid imagination. Her young son, she told the boy, was special. According to the story she created, she had found him in a beautiful gold box one snowy morning. She convinced him that angels looked out for him. The tales worked wonders. From an early age, Kirk said in *The Ragman's Son*, "I always knew that I would be somebody."

Herschel Danielovitch was the toughest man in Amsterdam, New York. He never lost a fight, and he got into them often. He was also an amazing storyteller. Kirk—who was named Issur at birth—was the only boy in the family. He had three older sisters and three younger sisters. Growing up surrounded by women, he was very conscious of his father as the only example of a man the sheltered young boy had.

When Issur was born, on December 9, 1916, the family lived in a very poor section of town. Herschel barely made enough money to keep food on the table. Issur grew up speaking a combination of English and **Yiddish**, a language spoken by some Jewish people. By the time he started school, the family had changed its name to Demsky. His first name had been changed to Isadore, and he was often called Izzy. His sisters' first names were also Americanized. Pesha became Betty, Kaleh was Kay, and Tamara was Marion. The twins, Hashka and Siffra, became Ida and Fritzi, and baby Rachel became Ruth.

Young Izzy learned that new names could not change prejudice, however. He hated it when schoolmates jeered at him for being the son of a lowly ragman. Still, Izzy respected his father and wanted to be accepted by him. But Herschel never showed affection. He never rewarded his children with loving words, gifts, or money. Izzy was an industrious boy, though, and he made his own money by running errands for mill workers.

The Demsky family was not without problems. Herschel was a hard man to live with, and sometimes he was abusive. As a result, Bryna and the children eventually lived apart from him.

When Izzy got through high school, he had very little money for college. Still, he was determined to better himself. One year after graduating, he hitchhiked to St. Lawrence University in Canton, New York. He told the dean he had only $163. The dean looked over Izzy's good school record and worked out a college loan for him. Later, Izzy made the college wrestling team. He went on to become president of the student body.

When Izzy discovered acting at St. Lawrence, he decided it would be his life's work. He got a summer job at the Tamarack Playhouse at Lake Pleasant, New York. There he met a struggling actor who had been given the name Mladen Sekulovich at birth, but now called himself Karl Malden.

10

After graduating from St. Lawrence on June 12, 1939, Izzy tried to get a scholarship at the American Academy of Dramatic Arts in New York, the oldest acting school in the world. It was not the school's policy to give scholarships, however. Izzy went back to the Tamarack Playhouse that summer. He decided that he, like Mladen Sekulovich, needed a new name. He chose Douglas for his last name. Someone suggested Kirk as a first name. His first thrill that summer was seeing "Kirk Douglas" listed on the theater program.

Kirk went back to New York City and enrolled in an acting school. He left after only three days, however, to attend the American Academy of Dramatic Arts. Amazingly, the AADA had decided to give him the money he needed!

The course at the AADA was a two-year program. Kirk learned all aspects of acting. One of his instructors was the famous teacher Dr. Charles Jehlinger—whom students called "Jelly" for short, but never to his face. Jelly was so tough on Kirk that the young man was brought to tears. Still, he learned a lot about acting. Kirk was determined to stick with Jelly. After all, many of Jelly's students, such as Spencer Tracy and Katharine Hepburn, had gone on to become highly successful.

It wasn't easy at the AADA. Only 80 actors out of the original 168 in Kirk's class made it to their senior year. But the ones who toughed it out usually did well in show business. Kirk met other actors who went on to become famous. One of them was a young actress named Betty Joan Perski, who had changed her name to Betty Becal, and later to Lauren Bacall. He also met a beautiful young actress named Diana Dill, who would one day make a big difference in his life.

After graduating from the AADA in June 1941, Kirk returned to summer stock. In the fall he got a job as a waiter and made the rounds looking for acting work. His first big break was a small part in a **Broadway** show called *Spring Again*. He was the first student in his AADA class to get a job on Broadway. He got other small jobs, but something cut his young career short. It was World War II. Kirk Douglas signed up for the navy, to fight for his country.

Kirk Douglas,
Movie Star and Father

While Kirk was at the Notre Dame Midshipman School in South Bend, Indiana, he was amazed by a *Life* magazine cover. There in a checkered blouse, carrying a parasol, was the young movie actress Diana Dill. "Hey, I know that girl!" Kirk exclaimed to his roommates. "And you know what else? I'm going to marry her!"

Kirk had dated Diana while at the AADA, but he hadn't considered their friendship serious. Now he did. He wrote her a letter in care of *Life* magazine. *Life* forwarded the letter to Diana's modeling agency in New York, and they passed it on to Diana. Kirk and Diana met in New York and began dating again. On November 2, 1943, they got married in New Orleans, Louisiana. After only a few months together, though, Kirk had to go to sea, and to war.

Luckily, Kirk did not take part in any major battles. He became seriously ill with **amoebic dysentery** and had to be shipped to a naval hospital in San Diego, California. It was there that months of mail caught up with him, and he learned that Diana was going to have a baby. She came to California to be with him. When it was learned that he might continue to suffer from dysentery, he was given an honorable discharge from the navy.

Kirk had served his country, but could do no more for now. He wanted to act. After all, his friend Lauren Bacall was in Hollywood starring in her first big film, *To Have And Have Not,* with Humphrey Bogart. But Kirk still had to recover from illness, so he and Diana returned to the East Coast.

They stayed rent-free in a mansion in New Jersey owned by Diana's wealthy sister. Kirk got a great role in a long-running Broadway play called *Kiss and Tell*. Then, at 10:30 A.M. on September 25, 1944, their son was born. They named the baby Michael K. Douglas. Diana wanted to name Michael "Kirk Jr." But a simple K was all of his name that Kirk would allow.

Kirk's big Hollywood break came through his friend Lauren Bacall, who had become a star with her first film. She recommended Kirk to producer Hal Wallis, who cast Kirk as Barbara Stanwyck's drunken husband in *The Strange Love of Martha Ivers*. Then Kirk returned to New York to star in a play called *Woman Bites Dog*. When it quickly closed, he was out of work. He and Diana returned to Hollywood. On January 23, 1947, their second son, Joel, was born. To pay the bills for his growing family, he signed with Hal Wallis at Paramount Studios to do one movie a year for five years. After several more films, he proved to be a popular actor.

Professionally, Kirk's life was looking great. At home, though, life was not so perfect. He and Diana were having a hard time getting along. One reason was that she wanted to act again but found it too difficult with young children to care for. Another was that Kirk was too involved with some of his female costars. The couple tried to compromise, and Diana went off to Santa Barbara, California, to film *The Hasty Heart* with Ronald Reagan, while Kirk stayed home with the kids.

Kirk decided to make some other changes, starting with his acting roles. He turned down a $50,000 part in a prestigious film for the MGM **film studio**. Instead, he starred as a boxer in *Champion*, for $15,000. When the movie was released in July

Kirk holds Joel as he waves at his fans. Diana and Michael look on.

15

1949, it was a surprise hit. Kirk and Diana's marriage, though, had become a failure. They divorced on February 8, 1950. Diana moved back to New York, taking Michael and Joel with her. Michael was only five, and his parents' separation upset him deeply.

Kirk Douglas was a successful movie star now, but his family life was a mess. He remembered how his mother had been unable to stay with his father because of Herschel's abuse, and how Bryna and the children had lived apart from his father for so many years.

Still, Kirk and Diana treated each other with respect, and the boys learned to live with the situation. When Michael and Joel weren't in school, they would travel from the East Coast to be with their father on movie sets and to learn about his business.

And what a business it was!

Kirk became one of Hollywood's biggest stars. The first of his three nominations for Best Actor was for *Champion*; this was followed by a nomination for his portrayal of an evil movie producer in *The Bad and the Beautiful* in 1952. In addition, he had become such a celebrity that his name was "above the title"—his name was the first credit shown on the screen at the beginning of a movie, even before the film's title.

Kirk dated many famous actresses, but the only one he wanted to marry was Pier Angeli, with whom he starred in the circus movie *The Story of Three Loves*. Unfortunately, Pier was mentally unbalanced. It took Kirk a long time to find out that she promised herself to many men.

While shooting *Act of Love* in Paris, Kirk needed an assistant. He was introduced to a woman named Anne Buydens, who spoke several languages. To his amazement, Anne refused the job offer at first. He persisted, however, and she took the job. But she would not date him, which again amazed him. Kirk learned that Anne had barely escaped with her life when the Nazi army invaded her native Belgium during World War II. He became fascinated by the beautiful, sophisticated woman. He got her a job on his next film, *Ulysses*. After they began a romantic relationship, Kirk introduced Anne to his ex-wife, Diana. To his surprise, the women got along well.

Kirk had been convinced Pier Angeli would become his second wife. Instead, on May 29, 1954, he and Anne were married in Las Vegas, Nevada.

Thoughtful, organized Anne encouraged Kirk to produce his own films. Her understanding nature was exactly what he needed. She was pregnant when Kirk went off to produce and star in *Indian Fighter* in Oregon. Anne didn't even mind that Kirk gave a role in the film to his ex-wife. In fact, Anne stayed behind in Beverly Hills and took care of young Michael and Joel.

The second film project Kirk chose for his Bryna Production Company was *Lust for Life*, about the painter Vincent van Gogh. He enjoyed the role tremendously. When Anne gave birth on November 23, 1955, they named the boy Peter Vincent Douglas, after van Gogh. *Lust for Life* brought Kirk his third Academy Award nomination. This time he was convinced he would win. Instead, Yul Bryner won for *The King and I*.

When the news came, Kirk was alone in a hotel in Munich, Germany. He was preparing to start a film called *Paths of Glory*. He got an Oscar, anyway—a present sent over by Anne. It was inscribed, "To Daddy, who rates an Oscar with us always. Stolz and Peter." Stolz was Kirk's pet name for Anne.

On December 14, 1956, Diana Dill Douglas married William Darrid, a theatrical producer and writer. Darrid turned out to be a fine stepfather for Michael and Joel, and the Douglases and Darrids surprised people with how well they all got along.

On June 21, 1958, Eric Douglas was born to Kirk and Anne. The four sons of Kirk Douglas spent time with both families, on both the East and West coasts.

Although he had a busy career, Kirk always found time to spend with his sons, Michael, Joel, Peter, and Eric (*clockwise from top*).

In 1962, Kirk became the 137th film star to put footprints and handprints into concrete at Grauman's Chinese Theatre.

The year that Eric was born, Kirk decided to produce and star in a film about Spartacus, a slave who had almost overturned the Roman Empire. The problem was, another studio was doing the same story—starring Yul Bryner! Kirk didn't know the meaning of the word *quit*. He hired Dalton Trumbo, one of the greatest screenwriters of all time, to turn out a **script**. While the script was being written, Kirk did *The Devil's Disciple* in England with the legendary actor Laurence Olivier. He convinced Olivier and other top actors to be in *Spartacus*. When they learned what Kirk had done, the other studio abandoned its film with Yul Bryner.

When *Spartacus* opened in October 1960, it became a world-wide hit. Kirk Douglas had won no Oscars, but he was definitely a superstar. President John F. Kennedy and his brother Bobby loved the film. They invited Kirk to represent the United States at a film festival in Colombia. It was the first of many such visits Kirk paid on behalf of his country.

Kirk made more great films. After the political thriller *Seven Days in May*, though, he wanted to return to the stage. He had found a book he loved called *One Flew Over the Cuckoo's Nest,* by Ken Kesey. He hired a writer to turn it into a play, and it opened on Broadway in 1963. Newspaper critics hated the show, but it played for five months anyway. It was not the gigantic success Kirk thought it could be. And despite his superstar status, no one was interested in financing a film version.

Cuckoo's Nest eventually became a film, but not for another ten years. And then, Kirk Douglas did not play the lead role of Randle P. McMurphy. Nor did he produce the film. That job went to his son Michael, and what a job Michael did!

Michael Goes Hollywood

When Diana Douglas married William Darrid, they moved to Westport, Connecticut. Michael attended private schools like the all-male Deerfield Academy in Massachusetts and Choate in Wallingford, Connecticut. When it came time for college, he thought of going to Yale, the prestigious Ivy League university in Connecticut. Then he saw a brochure on the University of California at Santa Barbara (UCSB). On it was a young man with a surfboard walking on a beach beside two girls. His choice was made!

Unlike his father when he was in college, Michael was not involved in sports. In high school he had captained the ninth-grade football team, but he gave up football after that. "They used to say, 'Douglas may be light, but he's slow,'" he joked in talking about it. He did not excel as a student at UCSB, either. After two semesters, the school suggested he take a year off to mature. He went back to Connecticut and got a job working at a gas station. He excelled there, at least. He was voted "Mobil Man of the Month" for his performance. Unfortunately, he was also hanging out with a bad crowd. He stole car parts and participated in other criminal activity but didn't get caught.

At this point, Kirk stepped in to influence Michael's future. He took him along to England and Norway to film *The Heroes of Telemark*. Michael was given a small acting role. Then they traveled to Israel, where Michael worked as his father's assistant on *Cast a Giant Shadow*.

Kirk was very supportive to Michael, and was always eager to give him tips on acting.

After a year abroad helping make films, Michael returned to college in Santa Barbara. It was the mid-1960s, and like many others of his generation, he began experimenting with alternative life-styles. He went to live in a hippie community, in an area called Mountain Drive, where he partied endlessly. Michael later said, "It was like retiring at age 21." Somehow, through all this, he stayed in college. Then, in his junior year, he joined the drama club and discovered acting. He moved away from his hippie haven. "Most of those people just weren't very happy," he reflected later. "It felt good . . . but you weren't *doing* anything."

After graduating in 1968, Michael moved to New York City to continue his dramatic training. He studied with Sanford Meisner at the Neighborhood Playhouse, then with Wynn Handman at the American Place Theatre. Only a few months after he arrived in New York, he was cast as a free-spirited scientist in the CBS Playhouse production of *The Experiment*. His performance won him the leading role in *Hail, Hero!* the first project of CBS's theatrical film production company, Cinema Center Films. In 1970, Michael starred in his second feature, *Adam at 6 A.M.* The next year he appeared in the film *Summertree*, which was produced by Kirk Douglas's Bryna Production Company. Then, in 1972, he did *Napoleon and Samantha*, a sentimental children's drama made by the Disney Studios.

Kirk visits with Michael on the set of his first film, *Hail, Hero!*

Like his father, Michael did **summer stock** plays and Off-Broadway productions when not working on films. It was a TV show appearance, however, that helped him make a career breakthrough. Producer Quinn Martin saw Michael in an episode of the popular TV series *The FBI*. Martin was so impressed that he signed Michael for the police series *The Streets of San Francisco*. Michael costarred on the show with his father's old friend from summer stock, Karl Malden. *Streets* premiered in September 1972. It became one of ABC's highest-rated evening programs, and Michael earned three **Emmy Award** nominations for his role.

While directing some episodes of *Streets*, Michael became interested in all aspects of filmmaking. He started his own production company, Big Stick Productions, and produced several short films. His real passion, though, was a project Kirk loved. Michael wanted to produce *One Flew Over the Cuckoo's Nest* on film. He obtained the movie rights from his father and began looking for financing. After several motion picture studios turned him down, he got the money from Saul Zaentz, the owner of Fantasy Records.

By then, most people thought Kirk was too old to play the lead role in *Cuckoo's Nest*. So Jack Nicholson got it. The movie won five Academy Awards—Best Picture, Best Director, Best Screenplay, Best Actor, and Best Actress—and made more than $180 million at the box office. Audiences couldn't help wondering whether Kirk would have won the Oscar if he had played Randle P. McMurphy as he had dreamed.

Michael's career took off when he was cast in the television series *The Streets of San Francisco* with his father's friend Karl Malden.

Michael listens to his father while filming a segment of the *Today* show at Kirk's home in 1979.

To Michael, life seemed almost too good to be true. He was becoming respected as both an actor and a producer, and he was dating the actress Brenda Vaccaro.

In 1978, Michael starred in Michael Crichton's medical thriller *Coma* with Genevieve Bujold, but he was equally in demand as an independent producer. For his next project, he chose *The China Syndrome*, about an attempted cover-up of an accident at a nuclear power plant. Despite his success as an actor and a producer, he was unable to raise enough funds to make the movie. Investors thought *The China Syndrome* was **uncommercial** until Michael teamed up with Jane Fonda and her production company, IPC Films.

Michael teamed up with Jane Fonda to act in and produce the movie *The China Syndrome* in 1979.

Michael married Diandra Luker in 1977 at his father's home in Beverly Hills.

The movie, starring Jack Lemmon, Jane Fonda, and Michael, came out in 1979. In an amazing twist of fate, a real-life accident at a nuclear power plant at Three Mile Island, Pennsylvania, occurred only a few weeks after the film was released. The unfortunate event created a box office bonanza. The film received Academy Award nominations for Lemmon and Fonda, and for Best Screenplay. The National Board of Review named *The China Syndrome* one of the best films of the year.

Before making *The China Syndrome*, Michael ended his eight-year relationship with Brenda Vaccaro. While attending a preinaugural party honoring President Jimmy Carter in Washington, D.C., Michael met someone new: Diandra Luker, from Majorca, Spain. Diandra was 20 years old, the daughter of a diplomat, and enrolled in her last year at Georgetown University's foreign service program. She spoke five languages and had traveled widely. She knew almost nothing about Hollywood, however. In fact, she had not even seen a movie until she was in her teens.

That didn't matter. Michael was smitten. Two weeks later, he asked Diandra to be his wife. They married on March 20, 1977, at Kirk and Anne Douglas's Beverly Hills home, less than two months after their first meeting!

On December 13, 1978, Diandra gave birth to Cameron Mitchell Douglas. At age 63, Kirk Douglas was a grandfather for the first time. Michael said that "after two years of marriage, including being a father, I know that my marriage is of utmost importance to me. Unexpectedly, marriage has helped me clarify my goals, assess my priorities, and work with more energy and effectiveness than ever before."

Despite this statement, the marriage was headed for trouble. Michael thought of his grandfather, Herschel, who was separated from his family. He remembered his own parents divorcing. Could Michael break the chain of trouble? He didn't see the upset in 1979, but it was coming. And it would come—at least in part—as a result of Michael's career.

Life at the Top

Several successful Michael Douglas films followed *The China Syndrome*: *Running* in 1979; Claudia Weill's feminist comedy *It's My Turn* in 1980; and *The Star Chamber* in 1983. In 1985, he landed the choice role of Zach, the dictatorial director-choreographer in Richard Attenborough's screen version of Broadway's longest-running musical, *A Chorus Line*. Michael had won an Academy Award as a producer, and was making film after film as an actor. None of his acting roles was providing any kind of remarkable fame, though. Then he found a script that he thought might do it. It was called *Romancing the Stone*, and it would change his moviemaking reputation forever.

Michael gained recognition as much as a producer as an actor. Here he is pictured with Cher after winning an Oscar for Best Producer.

An amusing romantic fantasy, *Romancing the Stone* came out in 1984 and was an immediate hit. Michael had been developing the project for years, buying the script from Diane Thomas, a waitress he met in Malibu, California. It starred Kathleen Turner as Joan Wilder, a romance novelist. Michael's friend from his New York acting days, Danny DeVito, played the feisty comic schemer Ralphie. Michael played Jack Colton, a reluctant **soldier of fortune**. The film made more than $100 million at the box office, and Michael was named Producer of the Year by the **National Association of Theater Owners**. *Romancing the Stone* was not his only triumph that year. *Starman*, a film Michael produced, was the unexpected hit of the Christmas season and earned an Oscar nomination for Best Actor for Jeff Bridges.

In 1985, Michael, Turner, and DeVito got together again for the sequel to *Romancing the Stone*, *The Jewel of the Nile*. It did well, but Michael was looking to do something dramatic, something for which he would be taken seriously as an actor. So, in 1987, he starred opposite Glenn Close in the extremely successful psychological thriller *Fatal Attraction*. That same year, for the first time, he played an out-and-out villain, in Oliver Stone's *Wall Street*. *Wall Street* earned Michael his first Academy Award as Best Actor.

Just as Kirk Douglas had built his reputation on playing tough guys, a Michael Douglas screen personality was emerging. Michael played tough guys, too, and not always good ones. In Ridley Scott's 1989 thriller *Black Rain*, he played a tough U.S. cop trying to find a killer in Japan. In 1989, he once again teamed up with Kathleen Turner and Danny DeVito in *The War of the Roses*. In this film, Michael's character starts off as a likable enough person but ends up as an out-of-control lunatic.

Kirk has followed Michael's career very closely and has enjoyed all of his son's successes.

Following *The War of the Roses*, Michael starred in David Seltzer's adaptation of Susan Isaac's best-selling novel, *Shining Through*, opposite Melanie Griffith. The movie got little attention from the critics or the public. Then, in 1992, Michael went back to playing characters whose morals are questionable. He starred with Sharon Stone in Paul Verhoeven's *Basic Instinct*. This thriller was one of the year's top-grossing films, and made Sharon Stone a star. Michael followed with a powerful performance opposite Robert Duvall in Joel Schumacher's drama *Falling Down*. This time, he played an out-of-work aerospace worker who begins attacking the people and things that annoy him.

By the time *Falling Down* was released, any film starring Michael Douglas could be counted on to deal with controversial subjects. In the 1987 hit, *Fatal Attraction*, Michael played a happily married man who becomes involved with another woman. The woman, played by Glenn Close, becomes **obsessed** with Michael's character. She ends up dead, but only after trying to kill him and his family. In *Basic Instinct*, Michael's detective character develops an intense romantic attachment to a woman he is investigating as a potential murderer. And in *Falling Down*, the character he plays reacts against troubling elements of society, but in a violent and illegal way.

In 1994, Michael continued to star in films with controversial themes. He took the role of a man who charges his female boss with **sexual harassment**. The movie, costarring Demi Moore, was based on Michael Crichton's number one best-selling novel *Disclosure*.

Michael with Glenn Close, his costar in the movie *Fatal Attraction*.

While starring in successful films, Michael was producing other movies. In 1988, he formed Stonebridge Entertainment, which later produced *Flatliners*, directed by Joel Schumacher, and *Radio Flyer*, directed by Richard Donner. That same year he produced the hit comedy *Made in America,* starring Whoopi Goldberg, Ted Danson, and Will Smith.

As early as 1984, Hollywood rumors had surfaced about Michael and Diandra having marital problems. The rumors began when Michael spent long months deep in Mexico making *Romancing the Stone*, with only one short visit by his wife and son. So, after *Romancing the Stone* was done, Michael tried to put an end to the rumors and improve his personal life by moving his family to an expensive apartment on Central Park West in New York City. Michael said the location was "about six blocks from where I grew up." Cameron entered school, and Michael and Diandra worked to make family life as normal as possible.

Michael filmed *A Chorus Line* in New York, but the sequel to *Romancing the Stone* was shot in Morocco. Michael was gone, once again, for several months. For any wife, long separations from her husband would be difficult. Making it even tougher, Diandra had to watch Michael appear in love scenes with beautiful female costars like Glenn Close in *Fatal Attraction* and Sharon Stone in *Basic Instinct*.

When Michael was nominated for an Academy Award for his performance in *Wall Street*, **tabloid newspapers** again reported that the Douglas marriage was in trouble. But his wife was with him in the audience, crying happily, when he accepted his Oscar. Whatever problems he and Diandra may have had, they have apparently worked through them.

Currently, he and Diandra reside in Santa Barbara, California, with their son, Cameron. It is a small coastal city, more than 100 miles away from the craziness of Hollywood. They try to live as normal a life as possible.

Michael takes time to relax at the Cannes Film Festival in 1990.

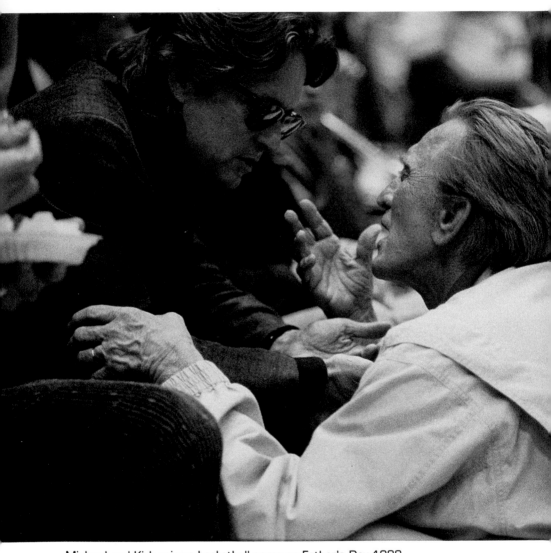

Michael and Kirk enjoy a basketball game on Father's Day 1988.

New Images for Father and Son

In September 1993, Michael Douglas was awarded the eighth American Cinematheque Award at a fund-raiser for this organization, which works to preserve films and videos of all types (the word *cinematheque* refers to movies). The award recognized his body of film work. Actress Goldie Hawn told the audience at the awards ceremony that Michael was "the most loyal of friends." Paramount Pictures chairwoman Sherry Lansing praised Michael on two counts. She said he had "hit-making ability" and never "played it safe." Jack Lemmon called Michael "a filmmaker with a social conscience."

And as for Kirk, the superstar father of the superstar son? In 1994, his career was still going strong. In fact, he had begun a brand-new career.

After his autobiography became a hit, Kirk began writing novels. *Dance with the Devil* was his first, followed by *The Gift*, then *Last Tango in Brooklyn*. His son Michael may have won the elusive Oscar, but Michael could not claim to be a best-selling author, too!

Kirk Douglas has enjoyed great success as a writer.

Kirk's film career was not abandoned, however. On March 10, 1994, the National Association of Theater Owners presented Kirk Douglas with its Lifetime Achievement Award. He had made over 80 movies, including one that came out shortly before the award. In *Greedy*, Kirk plays a mean old multimillionaire whose relatives scheme to get his fortune. It is a comic spoof on the dramatic tough guys he had become famous for playing.

While promoting the film, Kirk compared his career with his son's, in a talk with Bob Strauss of Los Angeles's *Daily News*. When Michael was about 22, I said to him, 'Y'know, you're way ahead of me. When I was 22, I wasn't thinking about the things you're thinking about.' He said to me, 'But Dad, when you were 22, you were just thinking of getting enough to eat.' He was aware of that. That's why he's a pretty good kid."

Kirk Douglas turned out to be a "pretty good kid" as well. Not long before *Greedy* opened, he and Anne sold a large portion of their prestigious art collection and donated the proceeds to charity. He and Anne had everything they needed and more, Kirk said, so why not give to those who were less fortunate?

Fortunate circumstances. Its mention brings us to an important question. Is it easier for the sons and daughters of superstars to make it in show business? Or is it tougher? In *The Ragman's Son*, Kirk Douglas wrote about the advice that he gave his kids about the entertainment business: "I advised all my children never to go into show business. It's such a poignant trade, the chances of success so remote. The definition of an actor—someone who loves rejection."

Kirk opened the 15th Cesar's French Film Industry award ceremony in 1990.

In writing about Michael's success, Kirk was proud that, in the Hollywood world of make-believe, his son "still has a sense of reality." He joked: "Of course, if I had known Michael was going to be so successful, I would have been much nicer to him when he was young. Be nice to your kids. You never know how they're going to grow up."

Despite the differences in their early lives, both Kirk and Michael Douglas overcame their difficulties to make it to the top of their profession. And unlike many who achieve such success,

Kirk Douglas has made over 80 movies in his long career as an actor.

both men have happy family lives. Any personal troubles seem to be in their past. And they both obviously love their chosen occupations. So what's their secret?

Kirk once talked about it. "There is no secret about it," he said. "You have to become your own critic and set a standard for yourself. There is no magical way. Follow your own instinct and hope that you are right."

Good advice, for a ragman's son, or for the son of a superstar.

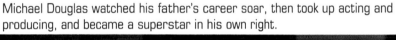

Michael Douglas watched his father's career soar, then took up acting and producing, and became a superstar in his own right.

Glossary

Academy Awards Annual awards given since 1927 to film artists and technicians, by the Academy of Motion Picture Arts and Sciences. The gold-plated Oscar statuettes awarded by the Academy recognize excellence in filmmaking.

American Academy of Dramatic Arts (AADA) A school for actors in New York City.

amoebic dysentery An infectious disease caused by microscopic creatures called amoebas. It causes inflammation of the lower bowels and diarrhea.

Broadway A street in New York City famous for its theaters. The theater district located on or near Broadway is regarded as the center of the theater and drama in the United States.

Emmy Award A statuette given annually by the National Academy of Television Arts and Sciences. The Emmy recognizes excellence in performances, production, and programming.

film studio Any building or collection of buildings where films are made on a regular basis.

illiterate Unable to read and write.

Lifetime Achievement Award An award given for excellent work during a person's entire career.

National Association of Theater Owners An organization of people who own theaters where feature films are shown.

number one best-seller A book that is first on a list compiled weekly by the *New York Times* and other publications.

obsessed Haunted by an idea, often an unreasonable one.

script A paper that describes, scene by scene, what takes place in a film. Scripts (or screenplays) have strict formats followed by anyone attempting to write a motion picture.

sexual harassment The act of making sexual advances toward someone who does not want them.

soldier of fortune A person who follows a military career for money or adventure.

summer stock Theaters where actors develop their talents in the summer, mostly doing plays that have already been successful on Broadway. Summer stock usually begins after June 1, and the majority of summer stock theaters are located in resort areas.

tabloid newspapers Publications such as the *National Enquirer* that report gossip which may or may not be true, usually about famous people.

uncommercial Describing a theatrical feature film that sells few tickets. In evaluating whether to make a film, investors consider how "commercial" it will be—how well tickets will sell.

Yiddish A language formed from a mixture of German, Hebrew, Polish, and Russian. It is written with Hebrew letters. Yiddish is spoken mainly by Jews who have emigrated from eastern Europe.

Index